The Fourth Trimester

The Fourth Trimester

And You Thought Labor Was Hard…

Advice, Humor, and Inspiration for

New Moms on Surviving the First

Six Weeks–and Beyond

AMY EINHORN

CROWN PUBLISHERS

NEW YORK

Published by Crown Publishers, New York, New York. Member of the
Crown Publishing Group.

Random House, Inc. New York, Toronto, London, Sydney, Auckland
www.randomhouse.com

Crown is a trademark and the Crown colophon is a registered trademark
of Random House, Inc.

Printed in the United States of America
Design by Lauren Dong
Illustrations by Merle Nacht

Library of Congress Cataloging-in-Publication Data
Einhorn, Amy.
    The fourth trimester: and you thought labor was hard...advice,
  humor, and inspiration for new moms on surviving the first six
  weeks—and beyond / Amy Einhorn—1st ed.
    1. Infants (Newborn)   2. Child rearing.   3. Parenting.
  4. Parent and infant.   I. Title: 4th trimester.   II. Title.
  HQ774 .E45 2000
  649'.122—dc21   00-055209

ISBN 0-8129-9106-0

10 9 8 7 6 5 4 3

For Ashley Rae

Author's Note

Some of you sharper-eyed grammarians may notice a "lack of agreement between subject and pronoun" in the following pages. In other words, I might write something like, "Your partner has to go to work, so it doesn't seem fair for them to have to be up at three in the morning." Yes, I may be a new mom, but no, I'm not brain-dead. I chose this construction for two reasons.

First, it's the way I talk, and we're just talking here. And second, it tackles that always tricky let's-not-assume-everyone-is-married-and-heterosexual-dilemma which today, I like to think, strikes any author of a certain evolved level. I know lots of moms who a) have male partners but are not married, b) have female partners who are not married, c) have female partners and are married, and d) have no partners. I wanted this book to speak to everyone. So I'm sacrificing some of the finer points of grammar to speak to all of the unshowered masses who are freaking out during their own Fourth Trimester.

And anyway, this book isn't about "partners" or "them." It's about us.

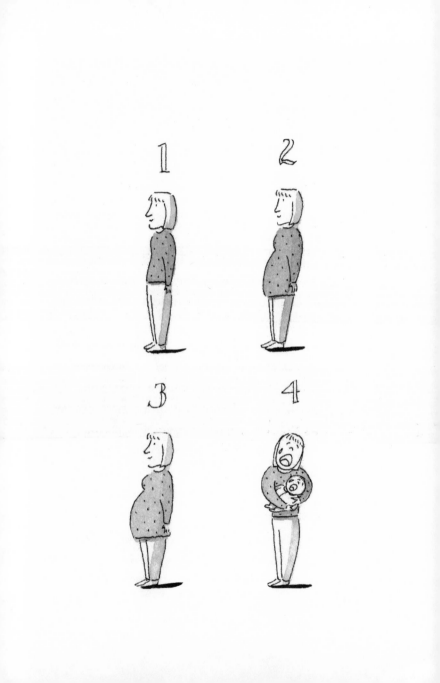

INTRODUCTION

You've learned that there are three stages to being pregnant: the first trimester, the second trimester, and the third trimester. During the first trimester, you have morning sickness; during the second, you buy overpriced maternity clothes, and during the third you look radiant (or at least everyone acts sweet and tells you that you do) while you waddle and wait.

But no one ever told you that there is a Fourth Trimester. The Fourth Trimester is that crucial period of time immediately after you've had your baby, when you are completely frazzled, adjusting to being a new mom. That's the bad news. The good news is that this Fourth Trimester lasts only around six weeks.

Why six weeks? A completely unscientific study of new mothers shows them picking hands down the first six weeks as the most difficult time. Perhaps because after six weeks you're getting the hang of it; perhaps because you've managed to fit into your old fat-clothes (you know, those clothes you kept around for those times you gained a few pounds); perhaps because the baby can finally do something beyond crying. For whatever reason, six weeks seems to be the magic number everyone decides upon.

I had my first baby when I was thirty-two years old. By this time I'd managed to lose the twenty-something pounds I put on during college, find a great guy who was willing to marry me without protesting too much, rise to a somewhat respectable position in a difficult field, and even to train for and finish running my first marathon. Having a baby? Piece of cake.

Ha. How wrong I was.

Now, I love my baby fiercely. We look like a walking Gerber's advertisement. But the first six weeks, well, they were utter HELL. Sure, friends of mine who had children *hinted* that the first couple of weeks were hard. So I wouldn't get any sleep? Big deal. So the baby would cry a lot? I could handle that. After all, I had exercised all during my pregnancy, taken Lamaze classes, and waddled into my ninth month without a hitch. I was prepared. I had read all there was to read about pregnancy and labor and even the toddler years. I'd read *What to Expect*...so I thought I knew what to expect.

What I didn't count on was being absolutely miserable and completely flipped out.

People asked if I ever thought I could love my baby so much. I'd nod and say yes, then swallow a big gulp in my throat. Every book I turned to talked about new mothers

10

being gaga in love with their newborn babies. I felt like a horrible failure because I wasn't feeling overwhelming love for my baby as much as I was feeling overwhelmed.

I remember one night during my first week home from the hospital. That afternoon I had called someone from a breast-feeding group on the phone because I was having trouble nursing. After listening to me explain how my right breast was cracked, bleeding, not producing any milk but only incredible pain, the woman on the phone told me ever so unpleasantly that I should be happy I could breast-feed on my left breast, that I could breast-feed exclusively on that one, and that I had to feed through the pain—then she invited me to come to one of her support groups (which incidentally I'd have to pony up money to attend). When I told my husband the story, he said, "You should have told her, 'Why would I come to one of your support groups when you're being so unsupportive and such a bitch?'" While my husband could at least think straight, I, being a new mother, was incapable of stringing together a coherent thought. Instead I figured this was one more mothering-thing I was a failure at. Three hours later I broke into tears while my parents, who had brought over Chinese food for dinner, looked on aghast with their forks of beef lo mein paused in mid-air.

Surely someone would have told me if it was supposed to be this way. I was obviously terrible at this.

However, as I spoke to friends of mine who were also new moms and going through the same experiences as me, I quickly realized that there is a stage of being pregnant that no one talks about—the Fourth Trimester. Just because the baby is on the outside instead of the inside doesn't mean your journey of becoming a mother is now over. The gestation period for a baby may be forty to forty-two weeks, but it takes an additional six weeks (at the very least) to become a confident, happy mom, or at least feel less like you're an imposter posing as a mom. By six weeks you may not be able to see the light at the end of the tunnel, and God knows you'll be up at all hours of the night where it's so dark you'll feel like you're living in a tunnel, but you will be able to tell which is the front end of the diaper without having to turn on a light.

Like me, you've probably read all of the books about pregnancy, labor, and parenting. But did you read anything about what was going to really happen to *you?* I'm not talking about you physically—we've all heard the stories about flabby stomachs and stretch marks. But what about your mind? Remember that advertising slogan, "A mind is a terrible thing to waste"? Well, aside from the obligatory postpartum entries and a paragraph or two telling you it's going to be tough, these books are a little less than completely candid. Shouldn't somebody be taking you by the hand (aside from your partner to help you out of bed) and showing you the ropes?

Well, here's a hand. And a shoulder to cry on. And a best friend to confide in. Because that's really what you need right now. You want someone who will tell you that feeling like a miserable failure for the first couple of weeks and even months of your baby's life is normal. In fact, it's a rite of passage. It's called the Fourth Trimester. And then you need a joke or two to let you know that it's going to be okay, and that one day you'll be able to look back on this and laugh.

You can read this book in one sitting (if you have the time, though if you have that much free time, God bless you and go get some sleep), or better yet, read just one of these entries a day. It's designed to be read in short, intermittent periods since that's all the time a new mom usually has. Hopefully *The Fourth Trimester* will make you realize that you're not alone, that what you're experiencing is perfectly normal, and that though it might not seem like it, it does get better.

So take a deep breath, put away any and all mirrors that might cross your path, and hang in there—you're going to be fine.

The Fourth Trimester

There's a reason they call it labor.

Recovering from labor is the closest thing most women come to recuperating from a heavyweight fight. Chances are you were pushing for hours on end, you didn't sleep a bit, and you feel like you've been run over by a truck. If you had a vaginal delivery, and an episiotomy or tearing to boot, you are going to be sore and in serious pain. If you had a C-section, you've had *major* abdominal surgery and you're going to be in more serious pain. This is very easy to forget. Just because people have them all the time doesn't change this fact. Since it bears repeating, again, you've had *major* abdominal surgery. Don't try to do everything—in fact, don't try to do anything. Just sleep, feed the baby, and get waited on hand and foot. Sooner than you would like, everyone will leave and it will be just you and the baby, fending for yourselves.

This is not a Tylenol commercial.

When I was leaving the hospital, I assumed I'd be getting some medicine to take with me. But when I asked my doctor for a prescription he laughed: "The medicine you're taking is so strong, you could fall down flat on your face on the sidewalk and you wouldn't feel a thing," he said. The painkillers they give you in the hospital are incredibly powerful. Take away all of the endorphins and hormones floating around, and the fact is, you're much weaker than you feel. It's easy to try and be a martyr and forgo the medicine, especially if you're nursing and nervous that the drugs will cross into your milk. Don't be a fool. You might have delivered without an epidural—okay, you are woman, we've heard you roar—now take some medicine if your doctor gives it to you and be kind to yourself. This is not the Olympics. While people might be impressed that you delivered without an epidural, no one's going to pat you on the back for a drug-free postgame show. Pain medication from your doctor won't hurt the baby (your baby will be taking Tylenol soon enough), and it will make your recovery a heck of a lot more comfortable. Recovering from labor is *painful,* whether you've had a vaginal or a cesarean. Remember, there are no brownie points for suffering.

𝒴ou will get no sleep in the hospital.

Maternity wards are actually set up to allow you the least amount of sleep possible. A possible reason for this is to delude you into the sensation that you are sleeping more when you get home with your newborn so you'll think you have the swing of things. When you come home, you will be exhausted. Try to get out of the hospital as soon as possible.

The milkwoman cometh.

You may have thought your breasts got big when you became pregnant. Well, when your milk comes in, you will look like you've developed grapefruits or cantaloupes (along with all of those little weird blue lines) for breasts. Except these babies will be rock hard.

It might seem that although your stomach has gone down, in fact, all that mass just made its way higher up and settled in your breasts. Wasn't it supposed to be what comes in must come out? Did someone forget that? The good news is that your breasts will get softer and go down (and down and down and down). So don't get flipped out if your bra size is somewhere so deep into the alphabet that you didn't even know they made bras that big. And whatever you do, don't rush out (or have others go out for you) and buy nursing bras during these first few days. This is temporary—your breasts will get softer, and smaller—so don't throw money down the drain buying bras that will only fit you for a week.

The other neat little surprise is not only do your breasts get huge, but when your milk comes in, they hurt like *hell*. Is it possible that it hurts more than labor? Yep. Unfortunately, they don't give epidurals for your milk coming in (though perhaps any doctors reading this should get to work on that). Again, this too shall pass.

If you are breast-feeding, it will hurt.

A lot. Chances are, if you are a new mom, you won't know what you're doing. Use the lactation consultants in the hospital. And if need be, pay for a private lactation consultant. It will be the best money you've ever spent (and you'll more than make up for it in the money you save on formula).

Yes, it might seem that all you need to do is whip out your breast, how difficult can it be? Very hard. And even if you know what you're doing, it takes time for your nipples to adjust from being sensory playthings to being pulled on and tweaked more often than a dairy cow's teat. You'll probably be tempted, *very tempted,* to give up. Especially after your first cracked nipple, first breast infection, or first clogged duct. (Helpful hint: Get your partner to massage your breast if you get a clog—it actually helps break up the clog, and they'll think it's sensual and that they're getting to cop a feel. It will be one of the rare times when you will allow them to touch your breast.) Oh, the joys of breast-feeding! But if you can stick with it, breast-feeding can be one of the most rewarding things you'll ever do. So think of it like everything else in life—coffee, beer, sex—at first it sucks (sorry) but eventually it gets better and better, to the point that you actually like it.

Did they forget the "maternal" in the maternity ward?

Some maternity ward nurses can be wonderful. But some can be downright mean. While the nurses on the delivery floor might be angels from up on high, unfortunately, often the nurses in the maternity ward are their counterparts from hell. They've seen a thousand babies, they know more than you do, and they love to lord it over you. They'll criticize how you hold the baby, how you nurse him, how you burp him. While you pick up your little darling every time he makes a noise, they seem to take their sweet time picking him up out of the nursery even though he's screaming his little lungs out and turning purple. Are they deaf? No. They're nurses, and this is just their job. Take what they say with a grain of salt and don't listen to everything they tell you. (No, you can't bottle-feed *and* breast-feed at the beginning, as one of them wrongly told my roommate in the hospital.) And whatever you do, don't expect to get compassion and sympathy from them—but as long as they keep the painkillers coming, God bless 'em.

Remember whose baby this is.

At the beginning, you will be doing everything wrong. Your mother and mother-in-law will give you helpful hints. This is, shall we say, the tip of the iceberg, a harbinger of the rest of your life as long as you remain on this earth. Your mom will insist the baby needs to put on the new bouclé sweater she bought because she can feel a draft even though the air-conditioning in the hospital broke down and it's a balmy ninety degrees; your mother-in-law will tell you to be careful of the camera's flash around the baby's eyes. Hard as it may seem to comprehend, they're only doing it because they care about the baby, not because they love to see you squirm. You're feeling **so** insecure about this mom-thing that your reaction to them is, shall we say, severe. After all, if they told you to vote for Donald Trump, you'd just laugh and shrug it off. However, since this is a subject about which they *supposedly* know something about, you think there's got to be something to what they're saying. The fact is, sometimes they're right, sometimes they're wrong. You're the mom, and though you might not feel like you know what you're doing, you've actually spent more time with your baby and know him better than anyone else (yes, although the baby probably looks nothing like you, you weren't just a cocoon; that time in the womb does count for something). Just remember that from this time onward, your interactions with your mother and mother-in-law will be even more strained than before you had the baby (I know, hard to believe). But don't worry—you get payback in free babysitting, which you soon will be so grateful for that you'll be looking forward to having your mom and mother-in-law over as often as possible (I know, hard to believe).

There's no such thing as a parenting expert.

Even the so-called "experts" will give you conflicting advice. "Have the baby sleep on its back." But doesn't that thingy you bought at the baby store that has some parents' award seal of approval on it show the baby sleeping on its side? Some will tell you to have the baby sleep in the bed with you, while others will say whatever you do, don't have the baby sleep with you. Your friends who just had babies seem to have read the entire section in the bookstore on parenting advice—and borrowed their cousin-who-is-in-med-school's physiology books as well—and can quote page numbers when reciting Penelope Leach. You, on the other hand, are feeling rather sheepish for only having read *What to Expect* and dipped into some other books here and there. Not to worry—hard as it is to believe, people have been raising children for thousands of years without books or parenting experts. So take a deep breath, count to infinity, and realize that if everyone agreed on one right way to do everything, life would be pretty boring, not to mention that the parenting shelves in the bookstores would be pretty bare.

What's so sanitary about sanitary pads?

"Sanitary pad" is an oxymoron. You may never have used a sanitary pad in your life, but this has obviously now changed. Forget your good friend the tampon and say hello to what feels suspiciously like a diaper.

While you haven't had your period in around eleven months, congratulations, it's all been stored up waiting to blow. You're literally going to be a bloody mess for some time—a gusher for the first week, and some women can be spotting for up to two months after birth. So reacquaint yourself with the sanitary pad counter in the drugstore. And have more respect for your mother and grandmother for whom OB was nothing more than two letters in the alphabet.

The only person getting on the scale should be the baby.

People will be bringing you lots of food in the hospital and at home. Chocolate, cookies, good stuff. While you always hear that having a baby will make you lose twenty pounds immediately, "immediate" is a relative term. You'll be tempted to weigh yourself right away to see that scale

you've been staring down every week at the doctor's office plummet back down into your old neighborhood. Well, don't weigh yourself until *at least* a week after you've had the baby. If you've had a C-section, you've been pumped with enough fluid to fill a small portion of the Mississippi. Although your baby might weigh upward of eight pounds, chances are you'll have only lost a couple more than that. This will be depressing. So don't get on the scale, and eat those cookies. While being a baby is the only time in your life when it's cute to have chubby thighs, having just *had* a baby is the only time in your life when you can be overweight without apology. You're no longer doing the baby any harm by eating junk (unless you're breast-feeding, but now the Best-Odds diet police won't arrest you for having a piece of chocolate cake), and no one's expecting you to be in a bathing suit anytime soon. So forget about Weight Watchers and enjoy that Godiva.

Everyone poops—including post labor moms, unfortunately.

While peeing may not pose too much of a problem (though it may sting or burn, especially if you've had an episiotomy or been torn), many women approach their first postbirth bowel movement with more trepidation than labor. Chances are it will not be as bad as you antici-pate—the thought is worse than the actual movement itself. After all, if you pushed out your baby, you will be able to push out the remnants of that horrible hospital food you ate, no matter how daunting an idea that may be.

If the thought of going to the bathroom terrifies you, ask the nurses or your doctor for some stool softener to help ease you back into your routine. Because your days of quality reading time on the toilet are over—from now on you're going to have to be quick, quick, quick.

If you had a C-section, the nurses and doctors are going to be asking you if you are having gas. No, it's not because they're strange, and it's not because your room smells. They want to make sure that everything is back in working order. After all that they cut through and messed around with in there, it's no wonder they're concerned.

The baby doesn't look like either of you, but does look like the love-child of Yoda and E.T.

No matter what anyone says, newborns are not pretty. In fact, they're downright funny looking. Many look like the children of Dan Aykroyd and Jane Curtin's Conehead family. Just think about how bad you feel having come through labor. Well, *they* were the ones whose heads had to be squeezed through ten centimeters.

Before your baby begins to come into her own look, she will be a bit like Madonna, adopting various guises: Cyclops, one eye open, the other closed; a Grateful Dead groupie—doing a weird little dance with her hands over her head and in front of her face as if she's tripping on acid; a chicken—just check out those scrawny legs. Don't worry, soon it will become apparent that your babe is, for better or worse, related to you.

At first she may look exactly like your husband. There's an old wives' tale that says that newborns start out looking like their fathers to prove paternity (which, come to think about it, isn't so off-the-wall)—but by a year, your fifty percent will be showing its face.

Ahoy Ahab!

The baby is gone, but your stomach looks suspiciously like whale blubber. At first you may be in awe at how flat it is compared with how huge you were before you gave birth. That marvel will soon turn into a morbid fascination with the wide expanse of your stomach. Somehow your abdominal region resembles a vast, rolling plain—a desert with peaks and valleys and no end in sight.

You need to think of your stomach like a giant batch of Silly Putty that's been stretched out to cover the entire Sunday paper. It will go back to its original size, but it will take lots of massaging in order for it to fit back in that little egg. Realize that this will take time—and time and time—but what it's not time for is starting a Pilates class or any extensive sit-up regime. Give your body time to readjust on its own—in a few weeks, when you're feeling better, you can always help jump-start getting your body back with some exercise.

Is it an innie or an outie?

Well, at this point it sure as hell looks like an outie. A bizarre way-outie. When you see pictures of beautiful babies, they don't have these weird plastic clips and blackening stumps sticking out of their tummies. That's because umbilical cords are weird and ugly. They are not magazine- or TV-friendly.

Your baby's umbilical cord will fall off, though it may seem like it will take forever. In the meantime, remember to clean it a few times a day with a Q-Tip and alcohol, and otherwise keep it dry. And don't worry if it seems like it's taking an eternity—one day you're going to wake up and change that diaper, and ta-da, no more umbilical cord, just a clean, beautiful belly button.

You still deserve smiles, just not as many.

The first time you go out without the baby, you'll realize that no one will look at you and smile. You are no longer pregnant, you don't have a cute baby attached to you, you are just a mildly plump woman just like everyone else. Resist the urge to run up to strangers and tell them you just had a baby.

I thought staples were for paper?

If you've had a C-section, it's not clear why you can't just take a staple remover and take them out yourself. And God knows it's not a comforting image that they used staples— for God's sake, staples!—to seal you back up. But you do have to go to the doctor to get your staples out. She may say it won't hurt, but it will, a little bit. But in comparison to labor and the exams to see how much you were dilated, this is the most fun you'll have had with your doctor in a while.

Father may know best, but he doesn't know a thing about being a new mother.

Your husband may have been your Lamaze coach, he may have cut the umbilical cord, but come on, you can admit it. Try as he might to be the sensitive New Age man, the fact is he still has a penis. And not to male-bash, but this means he's clueless. He has no idea what you're going through.

When I had my daughter, I overheard my husband talking to his friend, trying to explain what being a new dad was like. He said the one thing that had changed was—are you ready for this?—that he missed reading a novel. Now mind you, as he's talking, I'm standing there having not showered, not been out of the house in a week, with bleeding, cracked nipples, and dark circles under my eyes that looked as if I'd swam the English Channel without remembering to take off my mascara (had I been at the point where I cared enough to wear any makeup). My husband, on the other hand, hadn't missed a day of running, was going to work every day, and aside from not having enough leisure time for reading, was overall just dandy. If I'd had any energy, I would have hit him.

What I did instead was think that we had finally entered the great divide. This was it. This was what separated the wheat from the chaff, the good marriages from the bad. I had previously thought we had a great relationship, that my husband was a true partner with me. But now I panicked. Was it all a mirage? Was I delusional? Because clearly how could we be experiencing becoming a parent in such different ways?

Now to be honest, I missed reading novels too. Of course this was probably number 99 on my list of top 100 things that I missed doing. But my husband, for the most part, still had the other 99 things that I no longer had. He had his body, he had his sleep (pretty much), his job, his life.

And me? Well, I had my baby's life. And while my husband was clearly affected by the birth of our daughter, there was no way he could understand how her birth affected me. Perhaps it's because I was the one who had been with her for the past nine and a half months when she was in my womb, or that I was the one who was now with her every minute of the day, or that sometimes I missed feeling her swimming around below my stomach, or that I cried because I just wanted to go to the gym, but then I cried when I did because I didn't feel guilty, so then I felt guilty (did you follow that?). To quote my friend Kelly, my daughter's birth rocked my world—while for my husband, it sort of just jiggled it.

So don't be alarmed if your husband acts as if he's on a different planet from you—in a sense, he is. He's trying his best to bond with the baby and with you. But the only feedback both of you are probably giving him is crying—a lot. Give yourselves some time. If you had a good marriage to begin with, parenthood won't change that (though it will change other things, namely those that start with the letter S—sleep and sex, both of which you won't be getting a lot of). New parenthood is like boot camp—surviving it will be an experience that will bond you together for life.

Automatic drip isn't just for coffeemakers.

Whether it be spit-up, pee, tears, breast milk, vaginal discharge, or just the cold sweat you break out into every time you hear your baby cry in the middle of the night—as a new mom your life is suddenly filled with fluid of one sort or another. You're not going to have a dry day for months.

Left, right, or was it right, left?

If you are breast-feeding, unless you want to end up with one über-breast, you definitely want to trade off equally between breasts for feedings. Why do you need a reminder? Because you will be suffering from *New Mother's Alzheimer's*—the baby is sucking your brain cells right out of you. Under the law of conservation of matter, as his IQ increases, yours is decreasing. Forget safety pins on your bra strap or hair thingies on wrists, the best tip anyone ever gave me about breast-feeding was to take a ring and switch it from one hand to the other to remind me which breast I last fed on. A ring is something you'll always have on hand, even in the middle of the night, unlike a bra strap, and you won't have to take it off in order to take a shower.

Breast is not always best.

If you're bottle-feeding, everyone will try to make you feel terrible for not breast-feeding. All you'll hear about is how much better breast milk is for babies. Everywhere you turn it will seem as if superior breast-feeding moms are taunting you with their babies suckled to their breasts. Just remember, almost all of them had to put up with sore nipples and clogged ducts that made childbirth look like a walk through the park. You'll get your body back quicker than your breast-feeding colleagues who will be toting around an extra few pounds; not to mention the wear and tear you'll be forgoing on your breasts. And while breast-feeding moms are up in the middle of the night, you, if you are smart, are catching up on valuable sleep while your partner is giving your babe a nice warm bottle. Bottle-feeding definitely has its advantages. The majority of us were formula-fed and we're all okay (relatively speaking). In the end, everyone turns out fine.

Who knew that was down there!?

You may have taken biology, you may be incredibly sexually experienced, but chances are that you're going to definitely learn a thing or two about anatomy when cleaning your child's vagina or penis. You'll feel a little bizarre trying to clean between all of the folds in your daughter's labia or around your son's testicles, but someone's got to do it, so better it be you, right? And don't be afraid to get in there and clean that gook out—but don't use baby wipes; use a clean, wet washcloth (the wipes can be irritating). You don't have to do this every time you change your baby, but at night after the bath make sure nothing is hidden in those nooks and crannies.

It's only sleep.

I don't normally quote my father-in-law (and God knows how many ass-kissing points I'm going to incur by immortalizing him in a book), but these sage words were in fact spoken by him in reference to the middle-of-the-night feeding shift he took with each of his three sons. Yes, your partner has to go to work in the morning, and while you are on maternity leave you don't, so it doesn't seem fair for them to have to be up at three in the morning....But wait a minute. What you are doing—staying at home taking care of a newborn all day—is harder and more trying than any job in an office could ever be. So if your babe is up in the middle of the night for a good hour or two, wake up your partner and let them have their turn. It's never too early to start setting an example for your child that one of the most important lessons in life is to share. And if your partner dares to complain or refuse, remind them that if their boss asked them to stay up late to work on a report, they'd do it no questions asked. Well, in this home, during this Fourth Trimester, you're the boss.

Put on a happy face.

Elaine on *Seinfeld* said noncircumcised penises have "no face, no personality." If you decide to circumcise your child, or if you're Jewish and are having a bris, this is one of those instances where you're better off not thinking too much about what's actually happening. You can take some solace from the fact that this procedure has been taking place for thousands of years and men still seem to be inordinately fond of their bald-headed penises. It doesn't seem to have dampened their nerve endings one bit. Look, if *Saturday Night Live* could have a commercial of a Cadillac going over speed bumps with a mohel in the backseat of the car circumcising a baby boy, surely you can get through this too.

"I think we're home, Toto."

Your baby may sleep a lot in the hospital, but coming home coincides with his waking up to the world. Get used to this, he'll be waking up more and more, and most of the time not when you want him to. Newborns sleep a lot—just not when you do. This can be maddening to put it mildly. Some countries not adhering to the Geneva Accords rank sleep deprivation highest amongst their arsenal of torture tactics, and for good reason.

Human beings were not made to get by on only two hours of uninterrupted sleep at a time. When Helen Hunt and Paul Reiser had a baby in *Mad About You,* she turned to him and said, "Remember all those times before we had a baby when I said I was tired? I lied." You didn't know what the word "tired" meant before you became a new mom.

The womb has its own version of Daylight Savings Time, and it's the exact opposite of ours. For many babies, night is day and day is night. Like people who deprogram members when they leave a cult, your job is to reprogram

your baby into learning to sleep through the night. This will be a long and arduous journey. But for now realize that you are getting by on so little sleep that under normal circumstances you would be nonfunctional. You would be calling in sick to work and sleeping for three days straight. Since this is not an option, at least give yourself a break. And be thankful that there's under-eye makeup.

Wireless phones we love, but wireless bras?

If you're breast-feeding, you're going to be told not to wear underwire nursing bras. This is because for some women underwire can cause clogged ducts. Unfortunately, if you're accustomed to wearing underwire, nonunderwire bras will take some getting used to. It's kind of like learning to type on a computer and having to go back to a typewriter, not a Selectric but a 1950s one. At first the bra might ride up your back and you'll swear you won't be able to get used to it. But give it a week or two, and if it's still uncomfortable, try a different style or size. Finding the right fit, and style, of nursing bra is difficult, more so than it should be. The maternity stores usually only carry their own brand, while the department stores carry only one other. But don't give up hope. If you persevere, you'll find a bra you like and that likes you back.

Obsessive compulsive behavior.

New moms check to see if the baby is breathing—often. This isn't just listening to the baby monitor on the top volume constantly. That goes without saying. This is peeking in when she's sleeping, and if you can't hear her, putting your hand on her stomach to see that it's rising and falling. You may do this so often that you wake the baby. But with thoughts of SIDS running rampant in your brain, you'd rather hear a crying baby than nothing at all. When your partner, who peculiarly doesn't seem to suffer from this phenomenon, comes to bed at night, you will make them check that the baby is breathing, even if they just checked a minute ago. Nothing anyone can say or do will deter you from this. You are a new mom.

However, there will come a day when you are *so* tired, and the thought of a crying, woken-up baby will be *so* repellent to you, that you will convince yourself that, of course, the baby is breathing. You will try and go to sleep, but again, those letters S-I-D-S will dance in your head. You will feel guilty and go check on the baby. At some point this behavior will stop, though curiously, a correlation seems to exist between the baby's first trashing of your really nice sweater and the belief that the baby is fine.

Babies cry. It's their job.

This may seem self-evident, but it's truly amazing how much a little person's crying can throw you into a panic attack. Don't let your baby's cry go unattended, but if a full sixty seconds will allow you to get dressed after coming out of the shower, then get dressed. Your baby won't think you don't love him. And you'll be much calmer feeding him with your underwear on than dripping wet in a towel.

Another thing to note is that there's crying, and then there's *crying*. While a little pick-up-the-baby-and-pat-him-on-the-back might quiet down a baby who is a little fussy in the morning, there's another realm of crying in the late afternoon that has its own entry in the Universal Mother's Dictionary:

> *Crying-for-hours-on-end-crying: Crying-with-no-end-in-sight at a decibel level that continues to increase with time. Syn: witching hour, colic, sensory overload, entering the Twilight Zone.*

The witching hour—from four P.M. onward. It's hell. No matter what you try—rocking, feeding, patting—nothing will make your child stop crying. Sure, they might stop to listen to the vacuum cleaner, but how long can *you* take listening to it? And yes, they might stop crying to drink or nurse, but stop the feeding and their faces are already red and raring to go before you've even blinked. A lot of babies cry for hours on end. Just remember, every parent you now see with a toddler has lived to tell this tale. In fact, this crying routine may be the only constancy in your life for quite some time. The only other person who might be even more miserable than your little bundle of joylessness is you, the mom. You are perfectly within your rights to be upset by this. Crying is not a nice sound.

So when your partner walks in the door, you are perfectly justified handing off your screaming banshee as if he were a nuclear hot potato. Woman was not made to hear constant crying for hours on end without getting out of the house. You need to think of this as a baton relay race: you've run the first three laps, now it's your partner's turn to run the anchor leg. So hand off that baton and get yourself to Starbucks.

You'll cry too. That's your job.

Postpartum syndrome happens to the best of us. You are probably thrilled that the baby is healthy, that you are no longer pregnant, that you can roll over onto your stomach, but nevertheless you will find yourself breaking into tears for no reason, at all times of the day. It will seem as if someone has hijacked your mental faculties. You are not crazy, you will not throw your baby out the window, you are just hormonal. This is the one time when your partner and people around you will be understanding of such outbursts.

That said, postpartum is a ticket to hell for your mate. You've suddenly gone from a woman full of maternal instincts to a slobbering idiot, one minute so grateful to your partner for being so compassionate, the next minute full of rage because your life has been turned upside down while theirs hasn't. Being at home full-time with a new baby, postpartum depression or not, is difficult. You're bound to feel some sort of resentment toward your partner, no matter how helpful they may be. Add to this mix bone-crushing fatigue and a serious hormonal Molotov cocktail, and you have a nice recipe for a testing of your vows. Notice that most marriage vows have "in sickness and in health," not "in the throws of postpartum depression." As with everything else, the postpartum depression will pass—it should only last a week—at which time your mental faculties will be returned to you, safely, in more or less the condition in which they were taken. Your relationship, however, will definitely suffer some bruises as you both adjust to being new parents. Why should you be the only one to be scarred from the birth? But as corny as it sounds, as with scar tissue, a relationship that can survive the initial few weeks of a newborn is one that will be all the stronger because of it. But if the "baby blues" don't fade and you find yourself thinking that Ingmar Bergman is one hilarious filmmaker, get thee to a therapist pronto.

$\mathcal{S}$trike up the vacuum; I hear a symphony.

Babies seem to like things that adult human beings don't—
the sound of vacuum cleaners, swinging and bouncing
until your hips almost separate from the rest of your body.
Try and find something that will calm your baby that is not
dangerous to your health. When all else fails, feel free to
risk your health.

You are not Martha Stewart.

Do not have everyone come over your house to look at the baby all at once, including your relatives. Space them out. Your job is not to entertain and put out chips and dip. Your job is to be an exhausted new mom.

Flip off the feeding fascists.

To hell with La Leche League—if God didn't want babies to use pacifiers, She wouldn't have had man invent them. Use 'em and abandon all guilt.

We've come a long way—except when it comes to husbands and babies.

Remember the punch line to that old joke: "The food is so bad, and the portions are so small"? This seems particularly apt for your feelings toward your husband. Why is it that it seems as if your husband can do no right, yet you can't wait for him to come home? You ask him to change the baby and when he brings her to you, her shirt is on backward. The baby spits up on the couch and his idea of cleaning it up is to rub it into the couch with his hands. Yet pity the fool if he's even two minutes late from work.

Just realize that all of your pent-up frustration and resentment has now found its outlet. No matter how much you enjoyed being pregnant, chances are you envied your husband his nonexpanding waistline and glasses of wine at dinner. After all, you were the one whose body was a walking science experiment for the past nine months, and it's justifiable if you now feel like your term of martyrdom is due to expire—in about one second. Unfortunately, if you are at home on maternity leave and your husband is back at work, the fact is you're going to shoulder the bulk of the responsibility for the baby. Men may be doing more of their fair share of the household duties these days, and your husband may be doing a hell of a lot more than his father did, yet it still pales in comparison to what you're doing. While most men don't get paternity leave, you can help even the load. Bully for your husband if he's a card-carrying feminist, but whenever possible just make sure he's a baby-carrying, diaper-changing, midnight-feeding one as well.

You will feel let down.

Maybe it's because the sex of the baby isn't what you secretly wished for. Maybe it's because you ended up having an epidural after you swore you wouldn't, or because you are no longer the center of attention, or simply because it's over and now you have this screaming being to look after. All of a sudden being pregnant looks like a great gig, while this parenting thing doesn't. You are not a terrible mother. You are just normal.

Embrace Zen Buddhism.

You need to live in the here and now. You are no longer in control of your own destiny. This fact cannot be emphasized enough. This little person is now in command of your every moment. You cannot plan on anything. Every time you think he is about to go to sleep, he will be up for another two hours. Every time you think you don't have time to take a shower before he'll wake up and want to eat, he'll end up sleeping for three hours. Babies, like a long line of historical figures—David vs. Goliath, Napoleon, the Wizard of Oz—may be short in stature but carry a big stick.

Think like the French.

If you're nursing, stop freaking out over that glass of wine you just had. If the French can drink and smoke and turn out beautiful children that grow up to have such style, surely your healthy American diet will allow for an indulgence now and then. After all, just think of all the highballs, pills, cigarettes, and God knows what else our mothers had when they were pregnant. This isn't to say you should run out and down a six-pack of Bud, but remember to keep things in perspective. Call your doctor for a reality check.

The walking dead.

When you venture outside, you will see other new moms with angelic-looking babies sleeping in their Snuglis. You may think that these babies are always like this. Those moms are *real* moms, you will think. They have things under control. Do not be deceived. Take a closer look. Notice if you will the looks on these mothers' faces. They look suspiciously like those Stepford Wives—blank, unemotional, almost as if they shot up with Prozac, don't they? This is because they, like you, are on autopilot. Their babies, just like yours, turn into shrieking banshees once they are inside, and that calm look on their mothers' faces dissolves into pure terror. Being outside is sometimes the only balm that soothes a crying baby, even if it's snowing and twenty degrees. So fear not the outside appearance of the über-mom. Eventually, she has to go inside too.

Showering (or changing your underwear) before nightfall is overrated.

You will have at least one day where you will not have found time to take a shower. You are not incompetent, you are not disorganized. You are just a new mom. New moms do this. As with all new moms, your personal hygiene habits have not gone out the window—they've just taken a bit of a holiday. They will return.

Toss the to-do lists.

You will get nothing done. Whole days will go by and you won't remember what you did except feed the baby, change the baby's diapers, get the baby to sleep. Doing "nothing" takes a lot of time. But you've done more by not doing anything than you did in entire days at the office. And it's way more important than anything you've ever done at work. Remember that—it's easy to forget.

The thought of being alone with the baby is (a) terrifying, (b) electrifying, (c) all of the above.

At first, when everyone is helping you, all you might want is for them to go away. Especially if those people include your mother and mother-in-law, who seem to know how to push every hot button you and your husband have (of course they do, they helped wire you, after all). But when it comes time for it to be just you and the baby alone, all day, you're probably going to have very mixed feelings. On one hand, you might be terrified. After all, what do *you* know about taking care of a baby? How are you going to do everything alone, without somebody helping you? On the other hand, the thought of just the two of you, without anyone else around, sounds idyllic. You're not schizophrenic. Your virgin outing into unassisted motherhood is, like everything else, a mix of a lot of emotions. So don't feel bad if you have a panic attack the last day your mother is helping you, or right before your partner goes back to work. It's going to be difficult to get the hang of doing everything yourself, but it's also going to be divine having everyone out of your house and having your baby to yourself for a while.

Learn to eat alone.

Forget about eating dinner together with your partner for the first few weeks. This will not be feasible. One of you will have to hold the baby while the other one eats. This will not last long—in fact, as soon as the baby can hold her head up so that she can go in the bouncy seat, you will once again be able to have a dining partner. But for now, console yourself with the knowledge that this is temporary.

Learn to eat quickly.

Forget about taking more than five minutes to eat a meal. During the day, eating a meal that requires a fork will be an oddity. This will be a hard habit to break. For a long time you will shovel food into your mouth like the contestants at the annual Nathan's hot-dog-eating contest at Coney Island.

On the sixth day God created bouncy seats.

And on the seventh day She rested. The bouncy seat, and its close cousin the Swyngo-matic (aka the "Neglecto-matic"), are a godsend. They will literally save your life. With the bouncy seat, you can take the baby into the bathroom with you while you take a shower. You can put the baby down. You don't have to constantly hold the baby. God bless bouncy seats.

The Swyngo-matic often swings the baby to sleep. Usually this is a hit-or-miss enterprise. Either the baby will be in the swing and become transfixed by some distant object and drift off into a suspiciously similar-looking state that the drug Ecstacy has been known to induce, that will then evolve into sleep; or he will immediately protest violently and refuse to stay in it. But if it works, you've used up your luck for the day, so don't bother playing the lottery.

If you're looking for REM, go to HMV.

For a while the only dreams you'll be having will be day-dreams—and they'll be of sleeping more than three hours in a row. Forget about REM sleep. Sleep whenever you can. This should be your mantra, your holy grail. You should only have two purposes in life—to take care of your baby and to sleep. Everything else comes third.

Everyone will tell you to sleep when the baby does. However, if you're like most new moms, you'll quickly real-ize that this is the only time that you can get anything done. Many a wise woman has followed this wanton path only to regret it later. *Don't do it.* "But," you may counter, "the baby sleeps at weird times during the day when I can't fall asleep." Well, even if you don't actually sleep, sit on the couch, read something that doesn't have to do with your job or with parenting. Whatever you do, don't clean up the house, unload the dishwasher, do the laundry. If you were working at a grueling job, you wouldn't immediately come home and start to do housework. You would unwind first, give yourself a chance to relax. The same should be true now. You are doing the Everest of all climbs, the hardest of all jobs. You are a new mom. So if you can't actually fall asleep when the babe is, pamper yourself and try at least to relax a little bit.

Hand over your bank card.

Do not make any financial decisions. You are not to be trusted. This may sound illogical since you are in charge of taking care of an entire human being. There's a reason they call it Mother Nature—your natural mothering instincts are great. They're not great, however, regarding the real world when it comes to money. Therefore don't order that baby backpack you like from that cool designer—you won't realize that it alone weighs ten pounds and when loaded it will be so heavy you won't be able to lift it and the baby at the same time. Don't buy three of the nursing bras you just found, because you'll probably end up finding the style uncomfortable after one week. Wait a while before whipping out your Visa. The Fourth Trimester goes away, but your credit report is yours for life.

The new four-letter word.

You may have never discussed bodily functions before, but all of a sudden the word "poop" will become the most used word in your vocabulary, the most discussed subject between you and your partner. "Did he poop? What color was it? Was it big? On a scale of one to ten?" At first you might cringe to hear yourself utter such a cutesy name. When you were a child your parents might have taught you to call it a BM, but you, after all, are of an eminently cooler generation. That said, there's something a little incongruous about saying "shit" in front of your little angel. So you, like legions of other parents before you, will say poop. Don't worry—you won't end up speaking in baby-talk in front of strangers—at least not immediately.

Also, don't be alarmed if your baby's poops don't resemble yours. At first they'll look like black tar; then they'll progress to "mustard-colored," which can be anything from yellow to orange to dark green—but whatever color they are, they'll be completely shapeless. If you are breast-feeding, you might feel like you're running your own little science experiments or paint-mixing shop. The carrots you ate for dinner the other night will give your baby's poops a beautiful orange tint, while that salad will add a nice shade of green. And while the literature they

hand out in the hospital says you should expect between two to four poops a day, if you're breast-feeding you can double that. Don't worry—and don't rush out to buy stock in Pampers—the pooping will slow down as your baby gets bigger.

Diaper changes don't accrue frequent flyer miles.

Too bad, but since they don't, don't change diapers as soon as the baby poops—give them a good five to ten minutes more. Chances are she's not done yet, and as soon as you change the diaper, she'll either pee or poop on the new diaper, or most probably on you, within a New York minute. If you imagine hearing a cash register ring every time you change a diaper, you'll be better about this. If your baby has serious diaper rash, you obviously won't have this luxury, but here's a tip: instead of using the gooky, messy, and smelly A&D and Desitin ointments, which you can't ever quite wash off your hands and which have a longer staying power than your more odious perfumes at the department store counter, try a little olive oil on your babe's tushy. For some babies this works wonders.

Working nine-to-five sounds like a great gig.

It's okay if you want to go back to work. You are not insane. Work is all about routine. And lunches that require forks and knives with other adults who talk about things other than sleeping schedules. And clothes that don't have spit-up on them (hopefully). And meetings that take place at set times. (Who would have ever thought you'd miss meetings?) Having a newborn is all about having no routine whatsoever. Right now you crave your old life. Your maternity leave will get better—as the baby gets older he'll get to be more fun—so don't pack up your briefcase just yet.

Think like Diana Ross's wardrobe consultant.

No matter how many spare outfits you pack in the ugly diaper bag (why, oh why, are they either so ugly or, excuse us Kate Spade, so damn expensive?), throw in one more. Until you get the hang of things, your baby will coincidentally pee while you're changing her diaper, wetting everything on her, or poop through those terrible excuses for diapers that they call "newborn diapers." If you're traveling with the babe, pack a spare outfit for yourself as well—if she spits/throws up/poops on you (take your choice), you want to have something to change into. There's nothing more tragic (especially for everyone around within smelling distance) than a baby who is cleaned up and smelling like a rose being held by a parent covered in spit-up/throw-up/poop (take your choice). And lastly, bring along some Ziploc plastic bags, which come in handy for everything from storing poopy diapers until you can find a trash can to holding pooped-on clothes till you can get home and do a wash.

Go topless.

You know you've entered dangerous territory when maternity clothes start to look good. Nursing shirts are horrible. They're designed to be the least flattering things made. You should have a few shirts at the beginning while you're still self-conscious about feeding in public, but don't invest in a lot of them. They're ugly, they're expensive, and it's just as easy to lift up your shirt. Accept the fact that modesty is out, cleavage is in. While previously you might have been as chaste as a nun, that period of your life has ended. Your boobs are no longer a sexual entity attached to yourself. They are a food supply. The sooner you accept this, the sooner everyone else will as well.

Try as you might to avoid nursing in public, if you're going to nurse, sooner or later you're going to have to do it in front of other people, probably strangers. You can buy one of those nursing bibs that covers the baby's head and your breast. But frankly, it's the baby that needs a bib for spit-up, not you. These nursing cover-ups seem like an extension of those horrible maternity clothes with bows on them—we're not babies, why do they insist on dressing us like them? You're not engaging in an indecent operation that needs to be covered up. That said, if you're that uncomfortable about baring your breasts in front of people, do whatever it takes to make you feel at ease. Fling a baby blanket over the whole proceedings. At first you may need a cover-up to ease you into the land of bare breasts in restaurants. But don't be shocked if in a few months you're whipping them out in the middle of the mall without giving it a second thought.

Babies have gas.

No matter what. It's not your fault, what you eat, or which formula you give them. If you're nursing, you can try varying what you eat (avoid dairy, broccoli, cauliflower, and if that still isn't helping, wheat), and if you're using formula, you can switch brands, but accept the fact that babies are gaseous little things. (My Lamaze teacher commented on how odd it was that people tell nursing moms to avoid Chinese and Mexican food because it gives babies gas. As if mothers in China and Mexico don't nurse?)

What have I done? Did I make a mistake?!

"If a complete stranger had rung my doorbell during the first few weeks and said, 'Give me the baby, I'll give it a good home,' I would have gladly handed her over, no questions asked." So said my friend who had a four-week-old. If a similar thought passes through your mind, you are not disqualified from the Mother of the Year competition. People will ask you if you have ever loved anything so much in your entire life. Don't feel bad if you don't. It's not until your baby is somewhat of a person that it gets to be fun. But people, especially mothers of older children, forget what the first few weeks are like. Again, DO NOT FEEL BAD. In a few months you will be able to answer this question honestly, without feeling like a fraud.

Miss Manners never had a newborn.

Tell your mother and mother-in-law that they can write the thank-you notes themselves if they start to complain that their friends haven't gotten cards yet.

How much Baby Gap can one child have?

Wait a *very* long time before you return all your Baby Gap presents for credit—as soon as you come home from the store, you're bound to have more boxes waiting for you. Also, Baby Gap credit works in the adult Gap, and you're going to need some in-between clothes to wear before you can fit into your old clothes. Don't feel guilty about trading the baby's presents in for a few things for yourself. The babies will get their revenge when they become teenagers.

Catch-22: a children's story.

You spend inordinate amounts of time trying to get the baby to sleep, yet you also spend almost equal amounts of time trying to get the baby to stay awake while he's eating.

Let sleeping babes sleep.

Whatever you do, don't wake up the baby to feed him. No matter what you've read or what your doctor tells you about it helping to get him on a schedule, it won't. What it will do is put an end to the few peaceful minutes, or hopefully hours, that you were experiencing. Does your baby look like he's starving? No. He looks like a chubby baby who's sleeping peacefully. He'll let you know when he's hungry. Unless of course your doctor is concerned about your baby's weight—then do whatever she tells you to do. Otherwise, go take a nap.

TV is good for you.

You will watch excessive amounts of TV, especially *The View* (we love *The View*) and reruns of TV shows you swear you never liked when they originally aired but now seem downright brilliant. Concurrently, the amount you read about things not having to do with baby development or parenting will drop off dramatically. Realize that magazines, especially *People* magazine, will be your lifeline to the outside world. They'll allow you to stay current on those things that are truly important. ("What did Gwyneth wear to the Oscars?") Also, they can be easily read while nursing or feeding with a bottle.

Even *ER* isn't this scary.

Conscientious parent that you are, you will probably take an Emergency Safety CPR class for babies. This will scare the bejesus out of you. The instructor will tell you every possible thing that could go wrong. All of sudden your home will go from looking like a warm, happy place to a kamikaze course intent on bodily harming your child. The teacher might tell you stories of children who swallowed quarters, who fell off their changing tables, who choked on apple slices. They might refer you to people whose jobs it is to baby-proof your home. For a couple of hundred dollars they'll do what your neighbor's two-year-old will do for free—find every possible dangerous item that can be put in their mouth, toppled over, or gotten into. Just remember that it's these people's job to tell you these stories. They're not going to tell you that almost everyone that you know with a baby has stories of dropping their child—and the children are all fine, give or take a few SAT points. You do have to be more careful now, but don't go nuts—just remember they can't charge thirty-five bucks for a class on common sense.

Yes, you have to take it rectally.

You may have finished high school, you may have finished college, you may even have a degree in astrophysics, but you'll have no idea how to take your baby's rectal temperature. Have your mom/neighbor/doctor show you where that thing actually goes (and no, you can't get away with using the digital ear thermometer—keep it in the box, it's no good on infants).

You're a slowly moving target.

Everyone will give you parenting advice—whether you like it or not. Little old ladies on buses will tell you your baby is suffocating in his Baby Bjorn, your mother-in-law will tell you that in their day they put their children down crying and let them cry themselves to sleep (to which there are so many retorts it boggles the imagination), your mother will tell you (especially if you're breast-feeding and she didn't) that the baby is hungry and hasn't gotten enough to eat even though you just nursed her for forty-five minutes. Just remember that in their day, walking around with safety pins attached to Maxi pads was considered progress.

Comparison shopping.

When you're out with your child in her carriage, you may think that people are looking at him, thinking, "What a cute baby." I hate to be the one to break it to you, but what they're really doing is checking out what kind of stroller you have. Don't believe me? Look next time and see where their eyes are going. At your child's face? Or just above it, to the Maclaren label?

At what age can ADD be diagnosed?

He stops crying when you shake the rattle in front of him, but fifteen seconds later that no longer does the trick. Solutions may work for an entire day or an entire minute only to inevitably lose their magic. No, it's not ADD. In fact, it's just the opposite. You have to remember that babies have gone from the dark, calm environment of the womb to this cacophony of sounds and sights that we call the world. Sometimes they're just overwhelmed, sometimes they're tired, sometimes they're hungry, sometimes they need to burp, and sometimes they just want to be left alone thank you very much.

You're still fat—you're supposed to be.

You did just have a baby, after all. Don't even try to get into any of your old clothes. Sure, we all hear the stories about so-and-so who went home in her size four jeans. Those people are mutations. They are not normal. You are normal—which means you will not be able to fit into your old clothes for a very long time. And while some of those books say that you should lose all the weight in the first two months, they also said you should only gain two to three pounds in the first trimester. Two to three pounds? Give me a break. Each of my breasts gained three pounds. As someone who gained nine pounds in the first trimester and then went on to lose all of my pregnancy weight after *nine* months (after two months I was still a puffball), I feel qualified to say that anyone who tells you how much weight to gain or lose in a certain period of time is an idiot. Everyone is different.

Hold off on that rubber ducky.

Baths will continue to be scary for everyone—you, the baby, anyone watching—until your precious one can sit up. While you may have had visions of your baby frolicking in the water, splashing with his rubber ducky, at the beginning it's more like a miniature *Poseidon Adventure,* and come to think of it, your baby looks like a miniature version of Shelley Winters as well.

So what is holding up her head anyway?

A friend of mine in medical school used to amuse us with stories about some of the patients she would see in the emergency room. One man was so obese that when he disrobed and they examined him, they found a cheese sandwich hidden in the folds of his skin. Don't be surprised if something similar happens with your child's neck. Oh, excuse me, did I say neck? I meant no-neck. Newborns have no necks. Somehow this hasn't been medically documented, but all new mothers know that necks are a part of the anatomy that seem to grow later. Try as you might to wash under that neck, it will be easier to find

gold in a stream. Whenever your babe is in the bath, she will keep her chin glued to her chest. But when you have company, or better yet, when your mother-in-law is over, she will lean her head back to reveal what you would swear is a neck, albeit a very dirty one. You can develop techniques for getting your child to lean her head back. But as with everything else, they'll work for a while and then, little genius that she is, she'll figure them out and stop biting at the bait.

Newborns get bored.

Your baby may be a nightmare with you all day. But within seconds the baby becomes an adorable cooing Gerber poster child when your partner enters. Do not take this personally—it's just the excitement of a new face.

Newborns are boring.

Grandparents may burst into applause when your baby burps and videotape his naps as if they were Oscar-winning performances. But that's because they only see him in short doses; 24/7 is another story. You may look at the clock and wonder if it's broken. "When did time move so slowly? What am I supposed to do with him all day?" Don't be upset if you're going a little crazy alone all the time with little junior. Your baby has a limited repertoire. Two may be company, but somehow your baby isn't holding up his end of the conversation right now. It's okay to seek out a third wheel.

NM SKS NMS (New Mom Seeks Other New Moms).

Mothers' groups—everyone compares their baby, and baby gear, against everyone else's. They're good, they allow you to get out of the house and breast-feed without being embarrassed. But be prepared. The down side is that they're group therapy and fashion shows for frustrated moms.

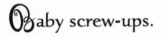aby screw-ups.

Everyone has 'em, but no one will admit to them (at least in front of their mother or mother-in-law). Rest assured that you are not the only one to have left your baby in a diaper for five hours and completely forgotten to change him; you're also not the only one to have almost poked the baby in the eye with your keys when he was in the Snugli facing forward for the first time; and you are definitely not the only one to have overdressed/underdressed your baby and not bothered to go back inside and change him since it is such a pain in the ass to get him undressed and then dressed again and since, as usual, you're already running late. The good news is…it will get worse! Once your baby gets more mobile he is a disaster waiting to happen. The changing table, which may have mesmerized and soothed him in the past (it was the only place my daughter stopped crying during her witching hours, leading my husband and me to try and see if we could make it her bed, though unhappily for us my mother said this was not an acceptable option), will now cause him to act like a mechanical bull trying to buck off every time you change his diaper—and he'll probably succeed once or twice. Unfortunately, if you haven't had them already, you are going to have a couple of major mishaps down the road. Hopefully they won't incur long-lasting damage or too many scars, physically and psychologically, for both of you. The sooner you accept this, the better. Your child will be blaming you for his hang-ups soon enough, no need to add your own guilt into the mix as well.

The joy (?) of sex.

At six weeks you can have sex again—this can be a good thing or a bad thing (but that's another book). For some the idea of having sex is so scary that it makes *The Exorcist* look like a Winnie-the-Pooh video. You may be thinking, If it took me a week after I had the baby before I was brave enough to go to the bathroom, how the hell am I going to have sex? Will the episiotomy come undone? Aren't I so stretched out that it will be embarrassing? Well, here are just a couple words of advice:

1. Think of yourself as a new virgin. If you don't want to, then don't. Wait until you're ready. Your partner has been getting on fine for the last few months with no intercourse; he can manage for a few more weeks.

2. While it may not hurt, it probably is going to be tender. Your first time back will not give Geena Davis and Brad Pitt in *Thelma and Louise* a run for their money.

3. *You will need lubrication.* Especially if you've been breast-feeding, it can be pretty dry down there. Almost as if she's in cahoots with the Pope, Mother Nature does this neat thing of not only using breast-feeding as birth control, but also making it incredibly uncomfortable to have sex if you decide to do it for reasons other than procreation.

4. If you've had a C-section, forget about the missionary position. Be like Nancy Friday—women on top, at least for a while.

5. Kegel schmegel, unless you've had a C-section (one of the few advantages of having a C-section), you're going to be stretched out.

6. If you wait until you have enough energy, you're going to be a grandmother. You are always going to be tired for the next few months. So if you've decided you are ready, to quote Nike, Just Do It.

Smile and the world smiles with you.

At six weeks your baby will smile, which makes it all worthwhile.

For the slightly less panicky,
but still sleep-deprived
next few weeks

To work, or not to work? That is the question.

You may not want to go back to work; you may want to; you may feel a little bit of both. For some women who don't have to go back to work, there is a choice. Wanting to go back to work doesn't mean you won't be able to be a Girl Scout leader for your daughter's Brownie troop. And wanting to stay home with your child doesn't mean Susan B. Anthony is rolling over in her grave. As you've probably realized at this point, as with everything else about parenting, nothing is black and white. Funny how you never noticed the world was really filled with gray.

If you have to work, even if you love your job, you'll be jealous of your friends who don't have to work. If you decide to stay home, you'll be envious of your friends who go to a job where they wear clothes with nonelastic waistbands and get real haircuts. Just remember, pretty much everybody, deep down inside, has conflicted feelings about whatever it is they choose to do—and if they tell you differently, they're lying.

Don't talk to strangers, unless they are your primary caretaker?

It will seem that everywhere you look, you see stories about day-care scandals. Friends will tell you about "friends of friends who installed a nanny-cam and guess what they found out?!" You may feel blind panic at the thought of handing over your child to someone else. You've known since the day you found out you were pregnant that you were going to have to go back to work. But knowing something intellectually, and now staring at this person (who is after all a complete stranger!) who is going to take care of your little darling is something entirely different. It's silly to make yourself crazy. Mothers have been working for a long time now. As a mother, your job is to do all the research you can, interview up the gazoo, check references, and then go with your gut. Remember, you only hear the horror stories because they're rare and because they tap into that phenomenon everyone loves to read, write, and talk about: *working mother's guilt.*

I may stay at home, but my IQ is still the same.

It may seem that all people ask you about anymore is the baby. It's not because they think you're no longer interesting now that you're at home. It's just because they can't think of anything else to talk to you about.

Pump it up, until you can't feel it.

No, Elvis Costello probably wasn't talking about breast pumping. But his song is truly apt for the subject. Pumping is not fun. It hurts. At times it may feel—and look—as if your nipples are being stretched so far out that they will tear off. A little known fact is that along with the stretching rack, the breast pump was a form of medieval torture used in the dungeons in all of those movies you've seen.

And don't think you are weird if you find yourself mesmerized by your nipples as they shoot out milk. There is something unbelievably hypnotic about it. You may sit down to pump and tell yourself you're going to read, that you're going to get through the pile of memos that's on your desk, only to find yourself fifteen minutes later with your eyes glued to your nipples. With all the talk

about the power of breast milk, somehow no one ever talks about the fact that pumping is absolutely mesmerizing as well. Remember, to your baby your breast milk is like opium, so it's not surprising that it's magical to you as well.

Have I turned into June Cleaver?

No, you haven't. Just because you're staying home with your child doesn't mean you've reverted back to a mom in a fifties sitcom. What it means is that you are lucky enough to be with your child all the time. This can be a blessing and a burden. The blessing part is that you actually have a standard of living. You don't spend hours commuting, being late to work, late to see your baby, feeling like you're short-shrifting both your personal life and your career. You get to be with your child more than anyone else. There's nothing that can compete with this. You know that commercial? "How much is that worth? Priceless." The burden part is when it's four o'clock, you haven't been able to go to the gym for a week, your partner won't be home for another three hours, and your baby is crying his eyes out and nothing, but nothing, will stop him. It's times like these that being stuck in a traffic jam with just you and a few hundred other cars seems like heaven.

It's no coincidence that the only people who know how to juggle are clowns.

Okay, okay, you've heard it up to here about juggling your family life and your career. And if you read one more article about a former CEO who quit her six-gazillion-dollar-a-year job to spend more quality time with her family, you're going to puke. Formerly the first one into the office, you're now late to work because you wanted to squeeze in one more feeding before you left her for the day. (She's so cute in the morning!) You then spend half the day worrying because you weren't able to stay up last night to finish that report because you were so tired from the three A.M. feedings that you fell asleep right after dinner. Are we having fun yet? No, probably not. But you have to take the fun in the short doses it's coming in—which means in the morning, at night, and on the weekends. These brief periods will become longer. And as you and your baby get more on a routine, and as you become newly acquainted with your job as a working mother, it will get much better.

Nothing puts a bad day at the office in perspective like coming home to your daughter and seeing her smile at you. While the bad day at the office isn't the best of both worlds, the smile part certainly is.

1%, 2%, skim, or express.

Can you believe women actually pumped at work before they had electronic pumps? These women were a very determined bunch and had very strong arms. Have you ever *tried* a manual pump? Churning butter takes less effort. Luckily for us, we have it easier. We can pump in style.

As complicated as breast-feeding is, pumping is even more so. That's because it introduces a whole new set of factors. For instance, when you're breast-feeding, you have no idea how many ounces of milk you're feeding your child. Once you start pumping, you'll become obsessed with how many ounces the left breast yields versus the right. You'll set goals for yourself, "I got 12 ounces yesterday, I'm shooting for 14 by next week." Getting ready for work every day will be like going to science lab. You'll have your bottles, your sterilized breast shields, your cooler packs. Will your baby thank you for all the time you're going to spend locked away hooked up to a machine? No. But you'll feel like you're doing something good for him.

And you are. And when he becomes a terror at fifteen and you're fighting like mad, it'll be a nice trump card to throw into an argument.

Run away from home.

If you stay at home, it's important that you find some time for yourself. I know, everyone tells you this, and in a perfect world you would, along with creating world peace and eradicating hunger. But even if you don't have the resources to get a sitter, try and find another mom you can trade off with. Even if it's just an hour a week, you need time that's just for you. And no, that time when the baby is napping doesn't count. You need to be outside of a five-minute radius of your child.

Define, if you will, your valuables.

Okay, so you've found someone to look after your little darling. You like her. You really do. So you're getting ready to go to work. "Better not let my diamond ring just sit there on the dresser. But wait a minute. Aren't I leaving her with my son?! How can I be worried that she'll take my engagement ring but feel perfectly comfortable leaving her with my child?" The answer is that you don't feel perfectly comfortable leaving your child with her. Like every other working mother, you're making do. It doesn't mean you should find someone else. And it doesn't mean you're a bad mother. It means you have conflicted feelings—which you should have. While you may shrug it off, it's a very hard thing that you're doing. So give yourself a break. You don't actually know this person very well. Once you do, you're going to feel comfortable not only leaving your child with her, but at times you're going to wonder if she can take care of you too.

Letdown. What the hell is it? How I felt after I had the baby?

When you breast-feed your child, you never really have to think about letdown. Your baby latches on and sucks, your milk flows. But somehow that warm feeling isn't exactly replicated when you're pumping. Somewhere between plugging in the pump, installing the tubing, the breast shields, making sure that the white membranes are inserted properly, double-checking the lock on your door, or at least trying to find a corner in the ladies' room—call us crazy, but it's not the same. It's therefore quite reasonable that you might have trouble experiencing letdown, especially if you're nervous and in a rush. You can try looking at pictures of your child, listening to relaxing music. But just remember that as with everything else, it's going to take some time to get used to this. But you will. Soon you'll be strapping on those breast shields, flicking on the switch for that pump, and for some women, relishing the time since it forces you to relax.

Beware, however, that as difficult as it may be to have letdown when you want it, like other things in the Fourth Trimester, you have no control over certain circumstances. Some women only have to be asked about their baby—to just hear their baby's name—to experience letdown. This may happen at inopportune moments. This is why breast pads were invented. Put them with your American Express card and don't leave home without them. After your body adjusts to being back at work and not nursing 'round the clock, your breasts shouldn't continue to spout leaks, but until then be prepared.

A room of one's own.

When a colleague of mine used to pump at work, she would put a sign on the door that said, YOU REALLY DON'T WANT TO COME IN HERE. If you have an office with a door you can lock, as with the law of the universe that governs everything, inevitably someone (your assistant who has the key) will walk in on you at least once. But if you have a door that locks—count yourself lucky.

If you're not so lucky to have an office with a door that locks, you will become unbelievably acquainted with every detail of the office bathroom. While at the beginning it might seem like it's hopeless—after all, how are you supposed to relax enough to have letdown while you're topless in a public bathroom?—after a little while you will actually relax enough so that you will be able to pump. You will also get to know the bathroom habits of everyone in your office, who washes their hands, who doesn't. While on one hand this is knowledge you could have done without, now that you have it, isn't it better to know? It's also interesting to see the reaction of your female colleagues. Some will give you an embarrassed smile and walk out without saying a word. Others will be incredibly supportive. They'll tell you horror stories of what they had to endure when they were breast-feeding. They'll cheer you on. "Good for you!" It's a breast-bonding sisterhood.

Of course, people will want to know what you're doing in there two, three times a day. Some people are comfortable just telling everyone what's going on, while some aren't. More often than not by this point you'll be fine telling anyone what you're doing, but be prepared—some of your colleagues, in particular your male ones, will act as if you're in fourth grade and you just told them Suzy from next door has a crush on them. They may love breasts, but when it comes to work and breast-feeding, they operate on a strictly, "Don't ask, don't tell" policy.

Staying at home all day with a baby is hard work.

Aside from those politically correct people who correct people when they say they no longer work—you do work, it's just at home—most people don't give stay-at-home moms their due. In the working world you get reviews, bonuses, your boss telling you a job well done. At home you get none of this. There's no human resources department giving you an orientation. There is no office policy. There's no supervisor giving you a review with constructive criticism (unless you count your mother and mother-in-law, but let's not). There's no paycheck. There are no rules. It is anarchy. Your baby son isn't going to say, "Thanks, Mom, for all that you're sacrificing. I really appreciate it." The only concrete feedback you're going to get from him is spit-up, throw-up, and poop.

Unfortunately, your partner, while appreciative of what you're doing, doesn't really understand just how difficult being at home all day is. They hear about the baby's two-hour naps, the walks outside, the first smile—you can see how it sounds like a great gig. And it is—it's the best show on earth. But it's also very isolating, frustrating, and scary.

So whenever you can be with another mom, go out. Even if it is freezing outside and all you want to do is stay inside, even if you are scared your baby will scream his head off in the diner, go out and do it anyway. Commune with someone else going through what you are experiencing. We have all seen mothers out with screaming babies, and you know what? Most people give them a break. Because they deserve it.

Whatever you do, do not compare yourself to other moms, or worse yet, your mom. Yes, your mom might have had five children with no help and she seemed to manage a hell of a lot better than you are doing with one. But you know what? Chances are your mom also put you in a playpen and let you cry your eyes out while she did chores around the house, fed you bologna filled with red dye, and had friends up and down the block who were at home doing the exact same thing she was, not to mention her mom probably helped out a lot since she lived nearby.

We come from a generation that has turned parenting into a profession that necessitates the right gear, the right philosophy, the right books, and a healthy dose of competition. But as a new mom, by now you know that the most important thing isn't what the experts say, nor what people think of you. Being a new mother isn't about any of that. It's about when you and your baby are up at four A.M. and you're holding him until he goes to sleep, and it seems as if you two are the only ones on the planet. And what a beautiful planet that is.

ACKNOWLEDGMENTS

I am fortunate to have had a wonderful support group of family and friends that saw me through my Fourth Trimester.

First and foremost, my parents, Ted and Ellie Einhorn, who seem to be campaigning for grandparents of the year. Whether it be taking off from work to look after Ashley Rae when her babysitter disappeared, or holding my hand while I burst into tears during those first few weeks, you have been amazing.

A close second, but not far behind, in order of appearance: my sister Jennifer Einhorn, who refused to leave the hospital nursery and sat guard so there would be no baby-switching shenanigans going on, and is keeping a list of all of our parenting mistakes for Ashley Rae to take with her into therapy in twenty years; Barbara Greenberg, who was "the" first babysitter and is a hell of a godmother; Abby Howe Heiman, who didn't just say "I'll watch the baby for you" but really meant it and followed through; Linda Futterman, whose help was invaluable; Stanley Futterman, who taught Ashley Rae how to hold up her neck starting on day one (do or die); Marnie Stetson and David Futterman, for keeping a 1-800 parenting hot line number open twenty-four hours a day and never making us feel like we were idiots; Dan Futterman, for joining the makeshift babysitter-substitute parade without a second thought; Michel Noel, the greatest babysitter a mother could hope for—we'd be lost without you; Freda Rosenfeld, the best lactation consultant in the

New York area; Kelly McDevitt Connors, Beth Egan, Stacey Keare, Rita Snape Criz, and Christy McDevitt for sharing their Fourth Trimester experiences and medical expertise; and Deb Krivoy, such a super aunt that she put the health of her niece's mom (me!) above that of her precious cats; Bruce Einhorn and Marcia Ellis and Nathalie for offering love and support from literally around the world; Jean Kunhardt and Fred Herschkowitz for their in-home visits and terrific advice and support, and to Eliza and Suzannah Herschkowitz, for their love and play dates—we hope Ashley Rae grows up to be just like you.

My literary agent Victoria Sanders deserves a medal for sitting through a meeting devoted exclusively to the trials and tribulations of breast-feeding and other Fourth Trimester–related issues without breaking into laughter or getting nauseous. My thanks also to her endlessly patient assistant Selena James.

I am extremely fortunate to have found a wonderful editor who immediately "got" the Fourth Trimester, Betsy Rapoport. I'd also like to thank her assistant, Stephanie Higgs, and everyone at Crown Books.

Finally, I'd like to thank my husband, Matthew Futterman, for his support, patience, and love. I definitely won the lottery.

ABOUT THE AUTHOR

Jackie Merri Meyer

AMY EINHORN lives in New York with her husband and daughter, Ashley Rae. After only a few weeks of the Fourth Trimester, she almost decided to cut her maternity leave short and return to her job as a book editor on the theory that coworkers were likely to have fewer crying jags, tantrums, and diaper changes than her newborn. However, a growing affection for her brand-new daughter, and a deep and abiding fear of milk letdown during meetings, persuaded her to tough it out. She was therefore able to witness the exact moment (4:03 in the afternoon, seven weeks after birth) that Ashley Rae turned from an efficient but less than personable poop and gas delivery system to an adorable, cooing baby. Amy and Ashley Rae are happy that both of their gestation periods—new mom's and baby's—are over.